TABLE OF CONT

Introduction

Conclusion

Introduction

"I learned that courage was not the absence of fear but the triumph over it. The brave man is not he who does not feel afraid but he who conquers that fear." —Nelson Mandela.

Courage is what everybody wants. It is an attribute of good character that makes anyone worthy of respect. Everyone is equipped with a certain level of courage which allows them to face their fears and take risks without losing faith. It is a personality trait that everyone possesses but it sometimes falters because of bad experiences or memories. Having courage is necessary to succeed in many situations in life from meeting new people to pursuing your dreams. But how can you develop courage and overcome your fears?

In this book, you will learn everything about developing courage and how you can use it to face challenges in life. So, grab this chance to know more about courage and discover the perks of developing enough courage to win any battle.

Chapter 1:

An Overview

Courage is not something that we are born with. It is a habit that we can develop and practice in our daily lives. Everyone is afraid of something. But, being courageous can let you face or overcome your fears in life even if it means you should sacrifice or take risks. If you think you don't have the courage to surpass all the challenges in life, well you are wrong. Life will never run out of challenges. They are already part of anyone's life. That is the reason why each one of you is equipped with the courage to win any battles in life. You may know about the existence of courage in your system, but think about how you face every fear in your life since you were just little. Isn't it courage or just your instinct?

Courage Defined

Courage is one's ability to confront pain, fear, uncertainty, intimidation, or danger. There are different types of courage, which may range from endurance and physical strength to mental stamina and innovation. Some of the types of courage are:

- **Physical Courage**: This is the type of courage utilised when facing hardship, physical pain, and the threat of death.

- **Moral Courage**: This is the ability of a person to act rightly when facing popular opposition, scandal, discouragement, or shame.

In several traditions, courage has the same meaning as fortitude. In the Western tradition, notable thoughts on courage came from philosophers including Aquinas, Aristotle, and Kierkegaard. In Eastern tradition, several thoughts on courage were provided by Tao Te Ching. Recently, courage was explored by the psychology discipline.

Attributes of Courage

Courage is what everybody wants. Most of you have heard or seen it in numerous stories or even movies.

History books have taught everyone how to be courageous. There may be different types of courage but you should develop more of it as this can give you an edge and may lead you to success. If you think you don't have enough courage, then spend some time knowing the different attributes of courage. These include:

1. Feeling Fear Yet You Choose to Act

Many people are afraid of something yet most of you choose to act instead of letting fear eat you. Courage is not the absence of fear but it is overcoming your fears. Keep in mind that true courage is facing danger whenever you are afraid.

2. Following Your Heart

Achieving all of your dreams may be impossible. But, in this world, your time is limited and you need to follow your heart and this is what you call courage.

3. Standing Up For What Is Right

It is not everyone that dares to speak against injustice. That is why it takes a lot of courage to stand up and speak for what is right. Courage will also teach you when is the right time to sit and listen.

There are other attributes of courage. If you want to be more courageous, then you start today. Everyone has the power to level up their courage. You too can develop courage, which you can use as your greatest tool when beating your enemies and other things that block your way.

Chapter 2:

Identify Your Strengths

For you to accomplish or succeed at anything, you need to have strengths. If you don't know your strengths, you might not be able to have the courage to face the challenges in this life. Strengths are not the things you think you are good at. Just because you are good at a particular thing, does not mean that it is your strength. For it to be your strength, it should be your passion too. The ability to identify your strengths is a valuable skill that can help you achieve your personal and professional goals. Knowing your strengths can increase your self-awareness, confidence, creativity, and happiness. But, what are the ways to know your strengths?

Ways to Know Your Strengths

Your strengths will serve as your fuel to develop courage. Strength will let you feel strong. If you are confused between your strengths and weaknesses, then here are some of the ways you may consider:

- ***List Down What You Think You Are Good At***

Listing down the things you think you are good at can help you determine your strengths. Even if you hate doing it yet you excel at it, this can be your strength. So, make sure to list down everything that you are good at because this will help you in the long run.

- ***Identify What Makes You Excited***

Everyone has his or her excitement in life. So, what makes you excited? Being excited about something you plan to do can be your strength. You have to take note that you should have passion for what you do for it to be a strength. If you like what you are doing and you excel at it, then it is your strength.

- ***Develop self-awareness***

Self-awareness is the ability to recognize and understand your own emotions, thoughts, behaviors, and motivations. Developing self-awareness can help you identify your strengths by revealing what makes you unique, what energizes you, what fulfills you, and what evokes praise from others.

One way to develop self-awareness is to keep a journal or a log of your daily activities, feelings, and achievements. You can use this journal to reflect on what you enjoy doing, what you are good at, what challenges you, and what feedback you receive from others. You can also use this journal to track your progress and celebrate your successes.

Another way to develop self-awareness is to ask for feedback from people who know you well, such as family members, friends, colleagues, mentors, or coaches. You can ask them to share their observations and opinions about your strengths, weaknesses, values, goals, and personality traits. You can also ask them to give you specific examples of situations where they saw you use your strengths or overcome your weaknesses.

- *Take Some Self-Assessment Activities*

A good way to know your strengths is by taking some self-assessment activities. There are numerous experts who offer such activities for free. You can try any self-assessment activity you want.

Just make sure that this would allow you to know your strengths.

Taking these activities may be a waste of time for others. However, some who are confused and don't know where to get started may consider these activities. Other than knowing one's strengths, self-assessment activities could also allow you to determine your weaknesses, which you can improve in the long run for it to be one of your strengths. Keep in mind that there are some weaknesses that can be the key for you to succeed at something. You just need to know how to use it wisely.

- ***Imagine your best possible self***

Another way to identify your strengths is to imagine the best possible version of yourself in the future. This exercise can help you visualize your goals and aspirations and how you can use your strengths to achieve them.

To do this exercise, take a moment to imagine yourself five years from now. Try to be as specific as possible. Ask yourself:

☐ Who would you be?

☐ What would be your strengths and how would you be using them?

☐ Where would you be?

☐ What would you be doing?

☐ How would you feel?

Write down your answers in as much detail as possible. Then review them and highlight the strengths that stand out to you. These are the strengths that align with your values and passions and that can help you create the future you want.

- *Reflect on your strengths*

Once you have identified some of your strengths, it is important to reflect on how they affect your life. Reflection can help you appreciate and value your strengths more and also identify areas where you can improve or develop them further.

Some questions to help you reflect on your strengths are:

☐ What are the positive impacts of these strengths on your life?

☐ How do these strengths help you overcome challenges or cope with stress?

☐ How do these strengths help you connect with others or contribute to society?

☐ How do these strengths make you happy or fulfilled?

☐ How can you use these strengths more often or in new ways?

You can write down your answers in a journal or share them with someone else. You can also use these answers to set goals or action plans for using your strengths more effectively.

- *Celebrate and leverage your strengths*

The final step in identifying your strengths is to celebrate and leverage them. Celebrating your strengths means acknowledging and expressing gratitude for them. Leveraging your strengths means using them intentionally and strategically to achieve your goals and enhance your well-being.

Some ways to celebrate and leverage your strengths are:

☐ Share your strengths with others and ask them to share theirs with you.

☐ Give yourself compliments or rewards for using your strengths well.

□ Seek opportunities or challenges that require or enhance your strengths.

□ Join groups or communities that value or share your strengths.

□ Teach or mentor others who want to learn or develop your strengths.

By celebrating and leveraging your strengths, you can boost your self-esteem, motivation, and happiness. You can also inspire and influence others to do the same.

Signs of Strength

Another way to know your strength is to be aware of its signs and these include:

- *Success*: This shows that you are effective in the activity you are doing.

- *Instincts*: Find things that you instinctively look forward to. Then, capitalize on them.

- *Growth*: You are growing once you can concentrate on a particular activity and time flies by.

- *Needs*: Several activities could make you tired, but they will give you fulfillment.

Once you have determined your strengths, the next thing that you need to do is to nurture your skills at it. Your strengths will only improve if you will continue nurturing them. If you will take it for granted, this might be your weakness in the long run.

For you to nurture your strengths, there are different things you can do. One of these is to be involved in activities wherein you can use your skills. With this, you will not just be able to learn more, but also you will have the opportunity to improve your strengths even more especially if you have competitors who you think are better than you. So, don't waste time on something that would not value your strengths. Nurture your strengths and reap its offered benefits.

Chapter 3:

Think Positively

Staying positive is not a simple job. More often than not, others encourage negative thoughts especially if they are emotional and could not handle things rightly. But what they don't know is that negative thinking will just complicate things and will never lead anyone to the right path. Every problem is like the subject of Mathematics, there is always a solution and it's maybe just around the corner. Thinking positively, on the contrary, can keep you going which could give you the courage to win any battle no matter how tough they are. It is a mental attitude that involves focusing on the bright side of life and expecting positive outcomes. However, that does not mean ignoring or denying the negative aspects of life, but rather making the most of potential challenges, trying to see the best in others, and viewing oneself and one's abilities in a positive light.

How to Think Positively

For you to be happier, you will need to think positively even when it seems your life is falling apart. Have you tried looking at someone who is always happy and wondered how did they do it? Their positive attitude and positive outlook on life are what draw them to others. Thinking positively can help you attain your goals in life. This will also make your life much easier.

Below are some of the tips you can consider to keep a positive attitude when things went wrong:

* ***Don't Just Exist, But Learn to Live Your Life***

Live daily like it will be your last. Passion and a positive outlook in life are contagious. If you will stay upbeat, you will find that some people want to be around you.

- ***Don't React, But Rather Just Act***

Do not wait until things go wrong. Be proactive and you should make things happen for yourself. Being reactive to your situation will not let get going. Life is what you make. You only have one try. So, take life as it comes. Then, make the most of it.

- ***Regardless of the Outcome, Don't Stop Believing as Everything Happens for A Reason***

Each situation has the potential for good even if it seems bad at that particular moment.

- ***Be Thankful for What You Have***

Those who are successful know that gratitude will get them further than dissatisfaction. There is nothing wrong with ambition. However, don't forget to thank for what you have right now. People who are not satisfied will end up thinking that they will never have the chance to get what they want.

- ***When Opportunities Come Along, Seize Them***

Do not neglect your responsibilities for you to chase your dreams, but do not pass on the opportunities that perfectly fit your life.

- *Have a Sense of Humor*

People want to be around people who have a sense of humor even during their unfortunate moments. Part of thinking positively is learning how to smile or laugh at yourself.

- *Remember That You Are the One Who Controls Your Destiny*

No one may deny your dreams except you. There is hope as long as you are not dead. You have unlimited potential even if you are not doing something in your life. So, why not jump in? Then, make it the life you desire.

There is no doubt that positive thinking is a hard task especially when things are not going right. But, it is not impossible to do. Just keep in mind those tips above and you will be heading to the right path.

Other Tips to Help You Think More Positively

There are other tips that can help you think more positively and these include:

- *Set Clear Goals*

If you don't know what you want to aim for in life, then you will never know where your journey is going. But, if you will set clear goals, then you will be able to give yourself fulfillment. So, set your goals and set a positive attitude.

- ***Form a Mental Picture of Your Success***

Forming a mental picture of your success may be ridiculous. But, this can inspire you to achieve all your goals. You will also be motivated to reach what you desire in life.

- ***Take Responsibility and Ownership of Your Life***

Do not blame others or challenges. Do not be a victim. You are your boat's captain and you are the one deciding where it goes. If you are not happy with your life, then make another plan and take action at the soonest date.

- ***Fake Your Failures***

If everything else fails, then consider faking it. If you are nervous, worried or doubtful, you can pretend that you are self-assured and confident. Smile and act as though you're professional, successful, and positive. You can fool others and your brain. With this, you will be able to be confident to be a positive person because you already know how it feels to be positive at anything.

- *Eliminate the Negative*

Consider using positive self-talk for overcoming the negative thoughts and doubts that creep into your mind. Eliminate your worries about obstacles and difficulties by thinking positively. You should not ignore problems. You should face them for you to have the courage.

Negative thinking may be an easy option because it's more comfortable and provides less challenge. Don't fall into this trap. Think positively as this can be the key to boosting your courage.

How Does Positive Thinking Benefit One's Health and Happiness?

Positive thinking can have a positive impact on one's physical and mental health, as well as one's overall happiness. Some of the benefits of positive thinking include:

- **Reducing stress**: Positive thinking can help reduce stress by eliminating negative self-talk and replacing it with more constructive and optimistic thoughts. Stress can have harmful effects on one's health, such as weakening the immune system, increasing blood pressure, and impairing cognitive function. By reducing stress, positive thinking can help prevent or alleviate these effects and promote well-being.

- **Improving physical health**: Positive thinking can also improve one's physical health by enhancing one's immune system, lowering the risk of cardiovascular disease, and increasing longevity. Positive thinkers tend to have healthier behaviors, such as exercising regularly, eating well, and avoiding smoking and alcohol abuse. These behaviors can contribute to better physical health and prevent chronic diseases.

- **Enhancing mood**: Positive thinking can also enhance one's mood by increasing positive emotions, such as happiness, joy, gratitude, and satisfaction. Positive emotions can improve one's quality of life and well-being by creating a sense of meaning and purpose, fostering social connections, and inspiring creativity and motivation. Positive emotions can also buffer against negative emotions, such as sadness, anger, fear, and anxiety.

- **Boosting self-esteem**: Positive thinking can also boost one's self-esteem by improving one's self-image and self-confidence. Self-esteem is how one feels about oneself and one's abilities. Positive thinkers tend to have a more realistic and favorable view of themselves and their strengths. They also tend to accept themselves for who they are and appreciate their uniqueness. Self-esteem can affect one's happiness, relationships, performance, and success in life.

Chapter 4:

Analyse All Points of View

One's point of view is his or her perspective about a particular story. Everyone has their views in life. It may differ depending on how you grew up or what experiences you acquired from the past. For instance, if you are always surrounded by people with a positive attitude and never embrace negative thoughts when troubles strike, you will become an optimistic person. However, if you grew with an opposite environment, you will likely be a person who is always negative about every step you take. In such scenarios, the difference in people's points of view matters. To be courageous, looking at all points of view is important.

Why Analysing All Points of View is Vital in Developing Courage

Facing the day-to-day challenges in life can be difficult. You need to have enough amount of courage to fight and surpass such obstacles. Every individual has different point of view and looking at points of view is important for you to develop courage. But, why should you look at all points of view if you are the one who is facing the obstacle and not them?

There are many reasons why you should look at all points of view. One of these reasons is that not all points of view are the same. Some situations in life may be easy for you while other scenarios may be tough for you even if people around you think it's simple. This difference is what draws you from others. So, if you think you are struggling in your current situation, then think about how other people have done just to get through it.

The importance of points of view to develop courage is that this allows you to see the brighter side of the situation even though others think that it is already the end of the world for them. Instead of losing faith, you will be motivated and inspired to surpass the situation because you believe that you have the ability to succeed.

The Benefits Involved in Looking at All Points of View

You may think that looking at all points of view may not be worth your time. But, there are benefits you could experience once you have done it:

- **Be Able to Differentiate Your Current Situation from Others**

One of the best advantages of looking at all points of view is that you will be able to differentiate your current situation from others. People from different walks of life have different situations to deal with. Some are tough while others can be easy. But, once you are in a certain situation and you think you can't do it, then better think twice and compare your situation with others who are also going through your situation as this can give you a difference.

- **Perspectives of Other People Can Serve As Your Motivation or Inspiration**

Another benefit of taking a look at all points of view is that you can use others' perspectives as your inspiration or motivation. If you think you don't have courage, then think of those who do their best to win their battles in life and fight against any injustice. Rather than losing hope, why not use some points of view to be motivated and inspired? Whether it is your first or second time dealing with a certain circumstance, no one can beat you if you have courage.

You may think that it is hard to make others' points of view, your motivation or inspiration. But actually, the process is easy. You don't have to change yourself just to be courageous like others. What you only need to do is to be like them. By imposing their good character in your system, you will be able to be as courageous as they are.

- *You Will be Aware of the Things You Should or Should Not Do*

Looking at all points of view can also give you the chance to be aware of things you should or should not do. If you think your situation is a hopeless case, then learn from other people's experiences. With this, you will determine which things you should prioritize.

- *Better Understanding of What You're Going Through*

More often than not, people think they are at their worst if they are facing some challenges. It is because they don't have a better understanding of what they are going through. You have to remember that everything happens for a reason and you need courage to face any challenge that may come your way.

- ***Being Able to Take Action Wisely***

Being able to take action wisely is a common problem for some because, in the first place, they don't have any idea when or where to get started. By taking a look at all points of view, anyone can be able to take action wisely as they already have clues on how others do their best to face obstacles.

- ***Lets You Think Positively***

Even if things went wrong, looking at all points of view will give you a realization. You will realize that life can offer you something better only if you have the courage to take risks and keep moving forward without thinking about any negative thoughts. Through the past experiences of some people, you will be able to think positively, which can lead you in the right direction.

There are perks involved in analysing all points of view. So, if you want to develop enough courage, then don't forget to bear in mind those things above because they can make a huge difference.

How to Analyse Points of View

There are several steps involved in analysing all points of view on a topic or issue. The following is a general guide that can be adapted to different contexts and purposes:

- Identify the topic or issue and the main question or problem that needs to be addressed.
- Conduct a preliminary research to find out the background information, the key terms and concepts, and the main points of view on the topic or issue.
- Select the sources that represent different points of view on the topic or issue. These can include academic articles, books, reports, websites, media articles, podcasts, videos, etc. Make sure to evaluate the credibility, relevance, and quality of the sources.
- Read or watch the sources carefully and critically. Take notes of the main arguments, evidence, assumptions, values, and biases of each source. Identify the similarities and differences among the sources. Look for any gaps, inconsistencies, or contradictions among the sources.
- Compare and contrast the different points of view on the topic or issue. Evaluate the strengths and weaknesses of each point of view. Consider how each point of view

addresses the main question or problem. Consider how each point of view relates to your position or opinion.

- Write a summary or an essay that synthesises and analyses the different points of view on the topic or issue. Use appropriate transitions, citations, and references to connect and acknowledge the sources. Use clear and precise language to express your position or opinion and to support it with evidence from the sources.

Chapter 5:

Possess Persistence

"No great achievement is possible without persistent work." – Bertrand Russell

Persistence is probably one of the great characteristics that a person may possess. This is the ability to be determined or achieve something no matter what hindrances they are facing. Having persistence will give you the courage to succeed even if others already quit in the middle of their journey. There may be different reasons why people quit, but regardless of these, their courage and persistence have driven them toward their goals.

One of the benefits of possessing persistence is that it can help you pursue your dreams and aspirations. Persistence enables people to keep working hard and stay focused on their vision, even when they face obstacles, criticism, or failure. Persistence also helps people to learn from their mistakes and improve their skills and strategies. For example, successful entrepreneurs, inventors, artists, and athletes often demonstrate persistence in their endeavors, as they do not give up easily and try different approaches until they succeed. Persistence can also help you overcome difficulties and adversities in life. Persistence allows people to cope with stress, frustration, and disappointment, and to maintain a positive attitude and outlook. Persistence also helps people to seek support and resources when they need them, and to adapt to changing circumstances. For example, people who have faced illness, poverty, discrimination, or trauma often show persistence in their recovery, as they do not lose hope and strive to overcome their challenges.

Developing Persistence

Being persistent is one of the characteristics you should develop if you want to reach your goals, get what you desire, and may even be a means by which you assert yourself in the face of difficult or stubborn people. The application of persistence on various tasks, goals, or interactions is often what set apart those who fail and those who succeed in life.

Many people have the capacity to set their plans and goals toward success. However, only a few succeed as they stick to work on their goals or plans until these are accomplished. Moreso, most people stop even before they take a step. Often, they let fear or doubts paralyze them from moving persistently. But, sometimes, others have motivation that is not firm enough for their goals to work.

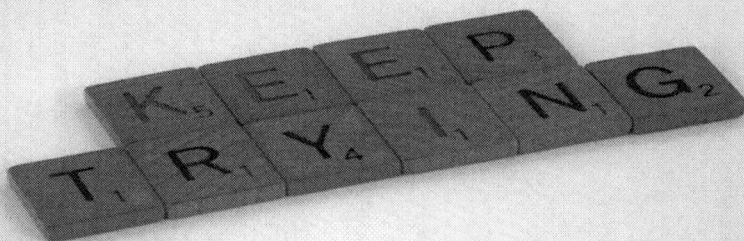

If you want to be persistent, here are some ways to develop persistence:

1. *Determine Your Wants and Desires*

If you do not have an idea of where you are going, then you will probably end somewhere else. Before you can successfully develop persistence and achieve success, you have to identify first your desires or wants. You can do this by writing down specifically all the things you like to accomplish or have. List down all your wants and desires even if some are impossible to achieve at the moment.

2. *Know Your Motivation*

Motivation comes from your deep reason why you want to achieve or obtain something. If you know why you are doing what you are doing, this provides you with more energy to keep moving. For example, you may like to publish a book. Creating books will take you time and patience. If you do not have enough motivation or a reason why you should publish it, you will probably never finish this. However, if you are motivated by the thought of teaching and influencing millions of readers through your words, only then you will push yourself hard to finish your book.

3. *Outline Your Action Step*

Determining your desires or wants speaks of what you want to achieve. Knowing your motivation will give you the reason why you want to attain your goals. Outlining your action step is important for knowing how you will be able to acquire what you want.

If you know how to acquire what you want, this will make it much easier to achieve. For you to know the steps, you should make some research and plan the things that should be done. Be specific on every step you want to take.

4. *Keeping a Positive Attitude*

The road to success is always under construction. It challenging to achieve success. This is the main reason why only some succeed. There will be many times that you will face failures especially if you are weak and your thoughts are full of doubts and fears.

For you to develop persistence and succeed in your journey, always keep a positive attitude no matter what the situation is. Keep your thoughts concentrated on taking some actions toward your goals. Avoid negative thoughts as well as feelings for this will just ruin your persistence and concentration.

5. *Build Your Group of Masterminds*

This group of individuals can help you succeed towards your goal. Pick carefully who you will trust because this may matter. If possible, include those who can offer you unbiased judgments and have a positive attitude. You cannot afford to waste your time listening to pessimists and cynical advice. These people will never help you succeed. But rather, they will drown your energy, which can lead you to failure.

6. *Develop Habit and Discipline*

All your planning and goal-setting will be just wasted if you will not be able to develop good habits and discipline. There will be tons of hindrances that will stop you from moving forward and without discipline, it won't be easy for you to sail away. Developing good habits and discipline can help you stay on the right track no matter what difficulties you are experiencing.

Chapter 6:

Step Outside Of Your Comfort Zone

Developing courage will require you to step outside of your comfort zone. This may seem easy, yet once you get there, coming out of your comfort zone is a bit challenging. We all have a comfort zone, a set of habits, routines and environments that we feel safe and familiar with. But sometimes, we need to step outside of our comfort zone and try something new, challenging or scary. Why? Because stepping outside of our comfort zone can help us grow, learn and discover new aspects of ourselves and the world.

One of the benefits of stepping outside of our comfort zone is that it can boost our confidence and self-esteem. When we face our fears and overcome obstacles, we prove to ourselves that we are capable and resilient. We also learn new skills and abilities that can help us in other areas of life. For example, if we try public speaking, we might become more comfortable with expressing our opinions and communicating with others.

Another benefit of stepping outside of our comfort zone is that it can spark our creativity and curiosity. When we expose ourselves to new experiences, cultures and perspectives, we broaden our horizons and stimulate our imagination. We might find new sources of inspiration, new ideas or new solutions to problems. For example, if we travel to a different country, we might learn about their history, customs and values, and gain a deeper understanding of ourselves and others.

A third benefit of stepping outside of our comfort zone is that it can make us happier and more fulfilled. When we challenge ourselves and pursue our passions, we feel more alive and engaged with life. We also experience positive emotions such as excitement, joy and gratitude. We might also find new opportunities, connections or purposes that enrich our lives. For example, if we volunteer for a cause we care about, we might make a positive difference in the world and meet like-minded people.

Ways to Step Outside of Your Comfort Zone

There are many ways to step outside of your comfort zone and these include:

* **_Learn Something New_**

Being in your comfort zone will limit your personal growth and development. Once you acquire new skills and have learned interesting stuff, you can have the chance to broaden your horizons. If you will learn another language, this can let you compete with other individuals. With this, you will be able to meet other people from different parts of the world.

* **_Travel_**

If you want something new, then try traveling. It is always a good and wonderful opportunity to come out of your comfort zone. This will enrich your life with your experience from other places. Traveling could also let you try different lifestyles, religious views, and cultures.

So, try breaking out of your shell. Then, embrace new cultures. This will let you live a whole new life.

* **_Do Things Alone_**

Doing things alone can be a great way for you to go outside your comfort zone. Being alone may sound strange, but this is normal. This will let you develop will and courage. This can also improve your confidence.

Stepping outside of your comfort zone may be difficult at first. But, consider taking small steps no matter what your experiences in life. Sooner or later, you will realize that you already have what you desire in life. It can be scary, stressful or risky. But it can also be rewarding, fun and empowering. The key is to find a balance between stretching ourselves and staying within our limits. We don't have to do something drastic or extreme to step outside of our comfort zone. We can start with small steps, such as trying a new hobby, talking to a stranger or taking a different route to work. The important thing is to be open-minded, curious and willing to learn from every experience.

Chapter 7:

Use Spiritually to Connect

Having the courage to face any trials in your life can let you stay on track despite the difficulties. But, without spirituality, most of you might lose faith to fight. This is the main reason why for you to have true courage you should also pay importance to the value of spirituality. Spiritualism is the search for something sacred and an important thing that people should take into consideration. People approach the realm of spirituality through meditation, religion, personal reflection or yoga.

Reasons Why Spirituality Is Needed to Be Courageous

Some people don't believe that spirituality has something to do with developing courage. However, they don't know that without this, a successful person can never be whole. That is why it is important to connect spiritually.

Below are the reasons why spirituality is needed to be courageous:

- ### *Spiritual Individuals Are Gracious*

Psychology demonstrated that expressing gratitude is connected with numerous positive emotions like overall vitality, being generous with resources and time, and optimism. Spirituality also encourages everyone to be positive which may be expressed in various life practices.

- ### *Spiritual Individuals Are Compassionate*

Showing compassion toward people is one of the attributes of people living a spiritual life. A variety of pro-social or positive emotions have strong links with spiritualism like letting one feel great about some things in life.

- **_Spiritual Individuals Flourish_**

Many said that spirituality is linked to numerous aspects of human lives. Those who are spiritual have positive relationships, are optimistic, have high self-esteem, have purpose and meaning in life.

- **_Spiritual Individuals Self-Actualize_**

People who have a high level of spirituality strive to get a better life. They also consider fulfillment and personal growth as their central goal. Spirituality is also considered as a path toward self-actualization.

- **_Spiritual Individuals Take Time to Savour Life Experiences_**

People who value spirituality take time to reflect on their everyday activities and build lasting memories of their experiences. Since spiritual individuals are more conscious about their activities, they learn to be contented with the small pleasures in life.

Being spiritual may be hard for some people. However, if you want to face this challenging world, you will need courage and spirituality to succeed.

Conclusion

Courage is a quality that makes us human and heroic. It is important in life because it allows us to face our fears, take risks, and seek our aspirations. Courage also allows us to grow as individuals, perceive things from new perspectives, and empower others. It is required for personal development, social transformation, and human advancement. Fear is a natural and healthy emotion that alerts us to potential dangers or challenges. Fear can also motivate us to prepare well and perform better. However, fear can also hold us back from taking action or trying new things if we let it. That is why we need courage to overcome our fear and move forward.

Identifying your strengths is a key skill that can help you achieve your personal and professional goals. Knowing your strengths can increase your self-awareness, confidence, creativity, and happiness. Furthermore, you can start by recognizing your fears, acknowledging them, and accepting them as part of the process of change. You can also use strategies such as breathing, mindfulness, positive self-talk, and seeking support to cope with your fear and reduce your stress. You can then choose to act courageously by taking small steps toward your goals, facing challenges, and learning from your mistakes.

Printed in Great Britain
by Amazon